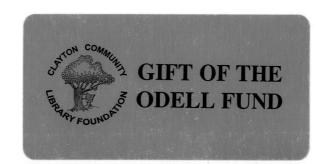

PREDATORS
LIONS

Sally Morgan

WITHDRAWN

 RSVP RAINTREE STECK-VAUGHN PUBLISHERS

A Harcourt Company

Austin   New York

www.raintreesteckvaughn.com

LOOK FOR THE PREDATOR

Look for the lion in boxes like this.
Here you will find extra facts, stories,
and other interesting information about lions.

Published by Raintree Steck-Vaughn Publishers, an imprint of Steck-Vaughn Company

Library of Congress Cataloging-in-Publication Data

Cataloging-in-publication data is available at the Library of Congress.

ISBN 0-7398-6602-8

Acknowledgements
The Publishers would like to thank the following for permission to reproduce photographs:
CORBIS Corporation/Images: pages 1, 2, 8, 8–9 top, 11 bottom, 12 bottom, 16–17 bottom, 19 bottom, 22, 29, 30; 4 bottom (Mary Ann McDonald); 5, 20 bottom (Yann Arthus-Bertrand); 17 bottom (Gallo Images); 23 top (Kevin Schafer); 24 top (Hulton Deutsch Collection); 25 (Wolfgang Kaehler); 26 (Charles & Josette Lenars); 27 (Richard T. Nowitz); 31 (Roger Tidman). Natural History Photo Library: pages 3, 4 top, 10, 16 (Stephen Krasemann); 14 (Andy Rouse); 9, 15 bottom (Martin Harvey); 11 top (Nigel J. Dennis); 12 top, 20 top (Jonathan & Angela Scott): 13 (Steve Toon); 18 (Daryl Balfour); 19 top (Steve Robinson); 21, 25, 28 (Christophe Ratier); 23 bottom (Norbert Wu). Papilio: pages 6, 7 top (P. Marazzi); 15 top (Dennis Johnson); 17 top (John Farmar).
Cover photos: Front cover: Ecoscene/Papilio/Joseph Boulter.
Back cover: CORBIS Corporation/Images.

Printed in China/Hong Kong
07 06 05 04 03
10 9 8 7 6 5 4 3 2 1

◀ Lions have powerful jaws and sharp teeth for killing prey (see page 12).

▶ A lioness stalks her prey on the African savanna (see page 16).

CONTENTS

KING OF THE JUNGLE

The lion is often called the "king of the jungle" because of its size and power. Lions are predators, or hunters—they eat other animals. The animals they hunt are called prey.

Another name for a predator is carnivore, or meat-eater. Lions belong to a group of animals called mammals, which are covered in fur or hair and produce milk for their young. Lions are cats, and they are closely related to cheetahs, leopards, tigers, and house cats.

▲ For the first few weeks of their life, young mammals, such as these lion cubs, drink milk from their mother .

▼ The adult lions allow the cubs to play, but they get a warning if they get too close!

Lions are found mostly in Africa south of the Sahara Desert, where they live mainly on flat grasslands known as the savanna. They live together in a small group called a pride. Within a pride there will be one or two male lions, five or six female lions, and their young. The young lions range in age from newborn to one or two years of age.

ONE TYPE OF LION
There is only one species of lion and its proper scientific name is *Panthera leo*. Most lions live in Africa, but a few live in northwestern India.

▼ Once the female lions have caught their prey, the other members of the pride come to feed.

KILLING MACHINE

A lion is a scary animal. It has a large and powerful body with lots of muscles. The male lion's job is to defend the pride, while the female is the hunter.

The body of the lion is perfectly designed for hunting and killing prey. The powerful body is strong enough to catch and hold onto prey and heavy enough to pull large prey, such as zebras and wildebeests, down to the ground. Lions cannot run for long distances. Instead, they run for a short distance at speeds up to 31 miles (50 kilometers) per hour. They can leap, too— as far as 29 feet (9 meters).

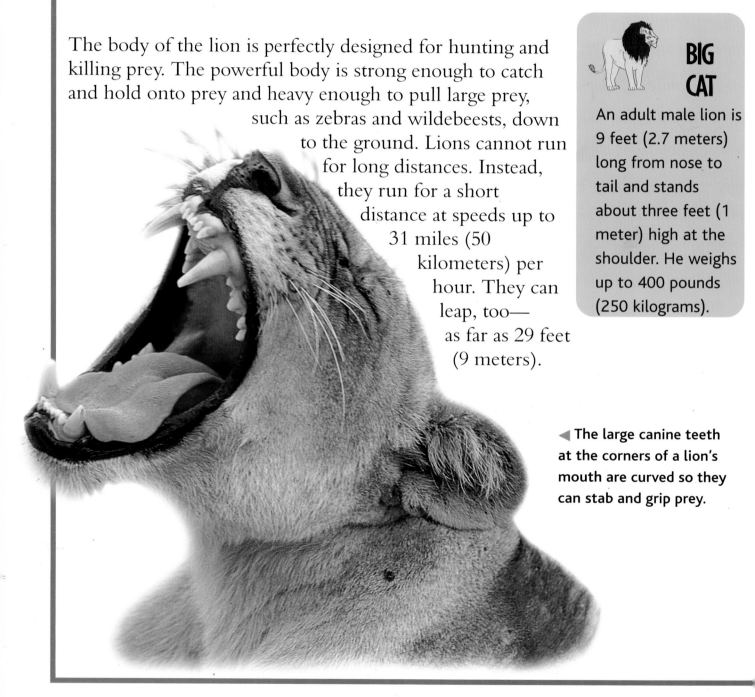

BIG CAT

An adult male lion is 9 feet (2.7 meters) long from nose to tail and stands about three feet (1 meter) high at the shoulder. He weighs up to 400 pounds (250 kilograms).

◀ The large canine teeth at the corners of a lion's mouth are curved so they can stab and grip prey.

▲ It is easy to tell the male and female lion apart. The male lion is larger and has a thick mane surrounding his face and covering the neck, shoulders, and chest.

The male lion is larger than the female. His thick mane of hair makes him look even larger. The mane starts to grow when the lion is about two years old and continues to get thicker throughout his life. Male lions are designed for fighting, so their mane protects their head and shoulders. The female is much lighter and, although she is not as powerful, she is better suited to hunting.

▶ This lion needs all her strength to pull down this prey. She will grip the animal with her claws and teeth.

GRASSLAND HOME

The savanna grasslands of Africa are home to herds of grazing animals such as antelopes, wildebeests, and zebras. These animals attract predators such as lions, cheetahs, and leopards.

For much of the year, the weather is hot and dry. The savanna turns golden brown during the dry months. As water becomes scarcer, herds of grazing animals move nearer to water holes and rivers where they can find water each day. The savanna looks very different during the rainy seasons. Once the rains have come, the grasses produce fresh growth, and the savanna is green again.

▼ A herd of zebra graze on the savanna. Most of the savanna is flat with a few flat-topped trees which provide shade during the long, hot summer.

THE SERENGETI

The Serengeti is a large area of savanna in Tanzania. During certain times of year, millions of wildebeest and zebra move across the plains in search of fresh grass. The huge number of animals means that there is plenty of food for lions and other predators.

Each pride of lions has a territory, or range, in which it lives. The territory has to provide the lions with all the food and water that they require. Territories vary in size from seven to 154 square miles (18 to 400 square kilometers), depending on the size of the pride and the amount of food available. The male lions patrol the boundaries of the territory. They mark trees and boulders with urine. Other lions will smell the urine and know that they are trespassing. The males of nearby prides may fight if they meet each other.

▲ This herd of buffalo includes a mother and her calf. The animals stay in a herd to protect one another against predators such as lions. They are just one of the many types of grazing animals found on the savanna.

▶ This is a Thomson's gazelle mother and calf. On the savanna, grazing animals tend to give birth at the same time of year— after the rains, when the grass and trees start to grow.

LION FOOD

Lions favorite foods are antelopes, gazelles, zebras, wildebeests, and their calves, but they will also eat small mammals, birds, and eggs. When they are hungry, lions will eat almost any other animal.

▼ This lion has caught a warthog and is carrying it back to the rest of the pride.

A zebra or wildebeest is large enough to feed the whole pride. However, lions do not catch large prey everyday, so they feed on smaller animals such as mongooses, impalas, dik-diks, warthogs, and even porcupines. When food is scarce they will feed on insects, fish, small birds, snakes, and eggs. When lions are very hungry, they scavenge on the remains of dead animals.

DAILY MEAT

Lions eat between 11 and 15 pounds (5-7 kilograms) of meat per day, but when there is plenty of food around, a lion may feast on as much as 66 pounds (30 kilograms) of meat in a single day. Then it may go days without eating.

◄ Since they are easy to catch, lone male lions prey on wildebeest calves. Lions hunting together will prey on both adults and calves.

▼ The hartebeest is a grazing animal that is found in small herds on the savanna.

Lions are thieves, too. If they have the opportunity they will steal food from other predators. Running after prey uses a lot of energy and there is a risk of injury. It is much easier to steal food from others. A lion may steal as much as half of its food from other predators such as leopards, cheetahs, and hyenas.

Hunting and chasing prey is very tiring. Once a lion has eaten as much as it wants, it will spend the rest of the day sleeping or resting in the shade. Lions may rest for up to 20 hours every day.

MIGHTY WEAPONS

The lion's main weapons are its claws and teeth. The claws are used to grip prey while the sharp teeth are used to kill.

A lion's claws are curved and sharp. They can be up to three inches (8 centimeters) long. They are extremely strong and are ideal for holding onto prey. Just like a pet cat, the claws of a lion can be pulled into the paws when they are not in use. This prevents them from being damaged or worn down. Also it helps a lion to walk silently on the pads of its paws. If a claw is lost, a new one grows in its place.

▲ A lion has four toes on its back legs and five on its front. Beneath each toe is a pad that acts as a cushion and helps to soften any noise as it approaches prey.

▶ The lion has strong jaws that can lock around the neck of its prey and suffocate it. It uses the weight of its body to stop the animal from struggling.

The short pointed teeth at the front of the mouth are called incisors. They are used to grip prey. Next to these are four extra-long curved teeth called canines. The molar teeth behind the canines have razor-sharp edges and are used to crush bone. These teeth can slice through tough skin and muscle. Lions do not chew their food. Instead, they bite off a large mouthful of meat and swallow it whole.

▼ The lion has 30 teeth. The canines stick out because they are longer and larger than the incisors. They are used to stab prey.

ROUGH TONGUE

A lion's tongue feels like rough sandpaper. This helps to grip prey. It is also good for pulling meat off bones.

LION SENSES

Senses are just as important to a lion as its claws and teeth. Lions use their senses of sight, smell, and hearing to locate their prey, especially at night.

A lion's eyes are excellent at detecting movement. When they see a predator, many animals remain still rather than running away. By remaining still, the prey is less likely to be seen by the lion.

RUBBING HEADS

Lions need to be able to identify members of the pride when they return after hunting. Lions greet each other by rubbing their heads together. This releases a smell that others will recognize.

▼ Lions have two forward-pointing eyes that give them good 3-D (three-dimensional) vision. This helps them to judge distances.

Lions have good night vision and often hunt at night. The black spot in the middle of each eye is called the pupil. The pupils control how much light enters the eyes. In bright light, the pupils are small. In the dark, they open very wide to let in as much light as possible so that the lion can see well enough to catch prey.

A good sense of hearing helps when the lion hunts at night. Lions turn their head in the direction of a sound in order to hear better. The sound of a lion roaring can travel over many miles. A lion uses its roar to stay in touch with other members of the pride and to let other lions know where it is.

▲ The lion's eyes are the largest of all the carnivores in the world. Lion cubs are born with eyes that are pale blue in color, but the color changes to amber as they grow older.

▼ This lion lies on a rock from where she can watch the grazing animals on the savanna.

GOING HUNTING

In the pride, it is the job of the female lion to hunt for food. Unlike other large cats, lions often hunt in groups. By working together, there is a better chance of success, and they can kill larger prey that will provide food for several days.

Lions cannot chase prey over long distances, so they try to get as close as possible before they start to run. A lion will creep slowly toward her prey, keeping low on the ground so she is hidden in the grass. Each paw is placed down silently. She may stop and listen to check that she has not startled her prey. This slow approach can take as long as 30 minutes. Once she is close enough, she will pounce or rush at top speed toward her prey.

▼A lion will approach her prey very slowly, creeping through the grass until she is within striking distance.

▲ Lions watch their prey from a high point, such as a hill, before deciding on the best approach.

When lions hunt together, they may spread out in a fan around the prey. Then they slowly approach their victim from several directions at the same time. Another method involves one or two lions rushing at the prey and pushing it toward other lions who are hiding. Some of the biggest prey animals, such as large buffalos, can only be brought down by several lions working together.

▲ Before they go off to hunt, lions lead their cubs to a safe place from where the cubs can watch the kill—and join the feast that follows.

SUCCESSFUL HUNTS

Even though the lion is a skilful hunter, only one hunt in five will end with a kill. Her prey often outrun her or see or hear her before she gets close enough to attack.

IN FOR THE KILL

Once a lion has caught her prey, she has to kill it. She uses her strong jaws and sharp teeth as her main weapons.

▼ This lion has started to chase her chosen prey, so all the other antelopes and zebras are galloping to safety.

STARVING CUBS

When food is short, many lion cubs will starve to death because the adults will not leave enough food for them. The adults are more concerned with their own survival.

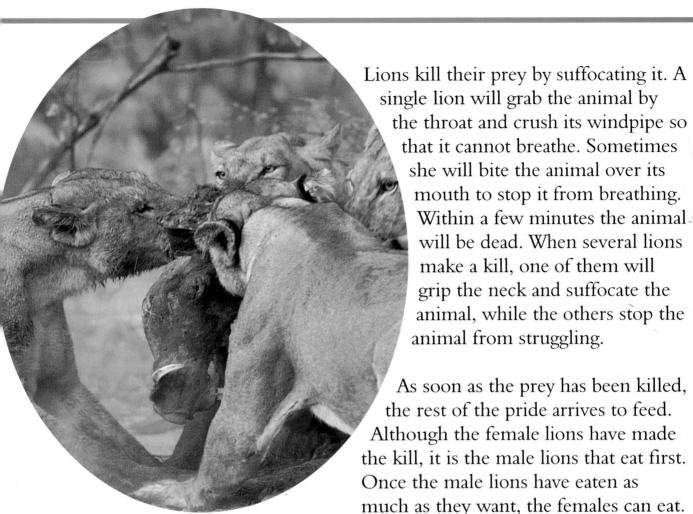

Lions kill their prey by suffocating it. A single lion will grab the animal by the throat and crush its windpipe so that it cannot breathe. Sometimes she will bite the animal over its mouth to stop it from breathing. Within a few minutes the animal will be dead. When several lions make a kill, one of them will grip the neck and suffocate the animal, while the others stop the animal from struggling.

As soon as the prey has been killed, the rest of the pride arrives to feed. Although the female lions have made the kill, it is the male lions that eat first. Once the male lions have eaten as much as they want, the females can eat. The cubs are the last to feed. Often, they have to make do with the leftovers.

▲ A warthog will not provide much food for four lions.

▼ A male lion will often steal a female's kill and feed on it first.

LEARNING TO KILL

Lion cubs have to learn to hunt. For the first year or two, young lions eat food that their mothers have killed. But they watch and learn and gradually get better at hunting.

A lion cub weighs about four pounds (2 kilograms) when it is born, and for the first few months the mother stays close and feeds it. Young lion cubs stay hidden in a den when the mother goes off to hunt. When they are two months old, they are introduced to the rest of the pride. Lion cubs of a similar age stay together in a nursery group. They are looked after by all the females, not just their mother.

▲ The rough and tumble of play helps lion cubs to become expert hunters.

▶ Cubs play with the adult lions, too. By playing, they learn some of the rules of the pride. If they break the rules, an adult will give them a slap.

Once they are large enough, their mothers will lead them to a kill where they can eat meat. Lion cubs love to play with each other. Play helps them to develop many of their hunting skills. They wrestle, tumble, and practice stalking each other.

When the cubs are about one year old, they follow their mother on a hunt. First, they are only allowed to watch, but later they are allowed to take part. They start hunting small animals and will not try to kill larger animals until they are about two years old.

▲ Lion cubs will be led to a kill by their mother, but they have to wait until all the adults have eaten before they can feed.

ENEMIES AND FIGHTS

A lion has few enemies. However, there are some animals that will challenge a lion for food. For a male lion, one of the biggest threats comes from other male lions.

The lion's main enemy is the hyena. Lions and hyenas hunt the same types of animals, so they often compete with each other. Fights over food are common. A group of hyenas will gather around a lion kill waiting for an opportunity to steal meat. But lions are just as likely to scare hyenas away from their kills, too.

◀ Elephants have little to fear from lions. Their large size and long tusks are good protection against lions.

BATTLING LIONS

When two male lions fight, they can inflict serious injury on each other and even death.

A mother cheetah and her cubs feed on a kill. Cheetahs are smaller than lions. If a lion comes across this kill, it will chase the cheetahs away.

Young females stay with the pride, but it is very different for their brothers. Young males are chased away from the pride. Some will wander around on their own, but most join up with their brothers or cousins to form a small group. Together, they can find food more easily. Eventually, when they are fully grown, they try to take over a pride by challenging a male lion to a fight. The winner will live with the pride, while the loser is chased away. Older males or sick males may be too weak to lead a pride, and they let younger and fitter males take over.

Hyenas will wait near a kill, hoping for a chance to steal some meat.

UNDER THREAT

Once lions were shot by people on big game hunts. Now they are shot when they stray onto farmland or come too close to people and livestock. But the greatest threats come from the loss of habitat and from disease.

In Africa there are large game reserves that give protection to all the animals living on the savanna. But this is not enough. In Africa the human population is growing rapidly and more land is being used to grow crops and to graze cattle, sheep, and goats. This means that the lion's habitat is disappearing.

▲ In the early 1900s, big game hunting was popular. Today most lions are protected, but in a few countries, this hunting is still allowed.

◄ Here researchers studying the spread of canine distemper in lions have tranquillized two lions that are suffering from the disease.

Disease is also threatening lions. Pet dogs get a disease called distemper. The dogs pass the disease on to hyenas and the hyenas pass it on to lions. In the Serengeti Game Reserve in Tanzania, the disease has killed more than 1,000 lions—that's one third of all the lions in the Serengeti. Research is underway to see if the pet dogs can be vaccinated against the disease to stop it from spreading any further.

▼ Many tourists visit game reserves in East Africa to see lions. Tourism brings a lot of money into the region, some of which goes into animal conservation.

THE ASIATIC LION

The Asiatic lion is an endangered species. It is found only in a small forested area of India. Fortunately the lion population is healthy, and there are plans to reintroduce lions into other forests. It is possible that Asiatic lions born in zoos may be reintroduced to the wild.

LION FACTS

ANCIENT LIONS

About 10,000 years ago, huge lions roamed parts of Europe, the Middle East, and the Americas. Although these lions no longer exist, their fierce reputation has lived on in legends, myths, and folk stories.

BEASTLY WARS

Two thousand years ago, Roman crowds used to watch prisoners and wild beasts, such as lions, fight to the death as a form of entertainment.

HEART OF A LION

In the Middle Ages, King Richard I of England was nicknamed "the Lionheart" because of his strength and courage. He led armies to fight in the Middle East, where lions were often encountered.

LION MEDICINE

Many people believe that lions have supernatural powers. They believe that eating lion parts can restore lost power, cure illness, and prevent death.

◄ A golden lion stands guard at the entrance to a Buddhist temple. Buddhists believe that the lion is a symbol of power.

MOTHER LOVE

A lion living in Kenya adopted a baby oryx (a type of large antelope). Park rangers decided to rescue the baby oryx because the lion could not feed her. Within a few months, the lion had found and adopted another oryx.

KING LION

Some African tribes believe that when important people in their tribe die, they are reborn as lions. In 1898, two lions killed many railroad workers who were building the Uganda-Kenya railroad. The workers refused to work, and all construction stopped. Local people believed that these lions were an ancient king and queen who had returned from the dead.

BORN FREE

One of the most famous lions of recent times was a lion named Elsa. Her mother was killed, and she was rescued as a cub by Joy Adamson. Adamson raised Elsa and released her back into the wild. The story of Elsa was featured in the film ***Born Free***.

▼ **This ancient stone carving shows a lion killing a wildebeest.**

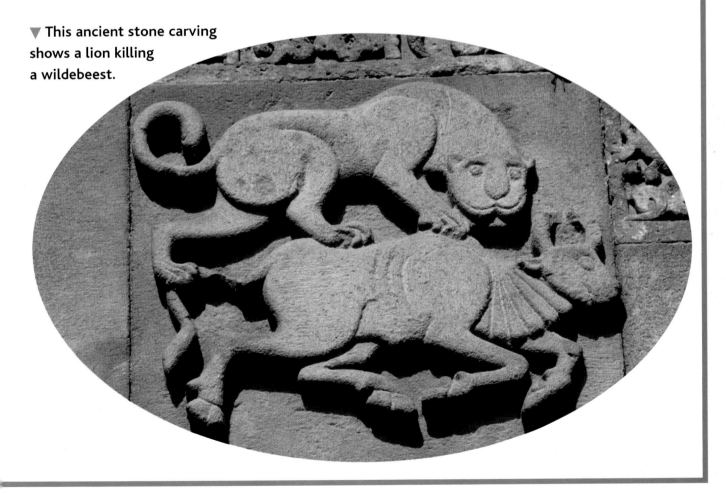

27

LION WORDS

This glossary explains some of the words used in this book that you might not have seen before.

Canine
large pointed tooth at the side of the mouth. A lion has four canines, two on the top jaw and two on the lower jaw.

Carnivore
an animal that hunts and eats other animals. Lions, cheetahs, and tigers are carnivores.

Habitat
the place where an animal or plant lives, for example a savanna or a rain forest.

Incisor
the small pointed teeth at the front of the jaw.

Mammal
an animal that produces milk for its young.

Molar
a large tooth near the back of the mouth used to crush food.

Patrol
to protect an area by walking up and down the boundaries.

Predator
an animal that hunts other animals and eats them.

▼ All mammals, including lions, produce milk for their young.

Prey

an animal that is hunted and killed by another animal—a predator—for food.

Pride

a group of lions that live together. A pride is made up of one or two adult males, several females, and a group of youngsters.

Savanna

tropical grasslands, where there are dry seasons and rainy seasons.

Scavenger

an animal that feeds on the dead and decayed bodies of animals.

Stalk

to creep up on something without being seen.

Supernatural

magical or mystical, something beyond the force of nature.

Territory

the area of land in which an individual or group lives.

Tranquilized

given a drug that makes one go to sleep for a short time.

Vaccinate

to inject an animal or a person with a drug that gives them protection against a certain disease.

Water hole

a pool of water that animals come to drink out of, especially during the dry season.

▼ **This lion is drinking at the edge of a water hole.**

LION PROJECTS

If you want to find out more about lions, here are some ideas for projects.

WATCHING LIONS

Not everyone can see lions in the wild, but you may be able to visit a zoo or an animal park that keeps lions. Take a notebook with you and make notes of what you observe. For example, watch where the lions walk and where they urinate or sharpen their claws. What do they do when they walk past each other? Do they sniff each other or rub heads? Study the differences between the males and females. Then compare the lions' behavior with that of other predators you can see at the zoo.

WHAT EATS WHAT?

Starting with lions, draw a food chain for wildlife on the Serengeti grasslands of East Africa. A food chain is a diagram linking each animal with the animals or plants it feeds on. The text in this book will give you some of the "links" in the lions' chain. To find more links, look at other books in your local library or look at some of the Internet sites listed opposite. See how many links you can make. Do any other African predators have similar animals and plants in their food chains? Are these predators competing with lions for food?

◄ Male and female lions look very different. The female has a slim, muscular body that is suited to hunting. The male lion has a heavier body, and his mane protects his head and neck during fights with other males.

The Asiatic lion is smaller than the African lion, and the mane is shorter and does not cover the ears.

PAW PRINTS

Lion tracks (footprints) can tell a field researcher where the animal traveled from and where it went. Trackers can tell how heavy the animal is and whether it is male or female, young or old, healthy or injured. You may not be able to track lions, but in muddy and sandy ground you could follow the tracks of other mammals such as deer, foxes, squirrels, or pet cats and dogs. Compare the numbers of toes and the size of the tracks.

HOW YOU CAN HELP

In the wild, lions are under threat. You can help protect them by supporting one of the many wildlife organizations that study lions and ensure their habitats are not destroyed.

LIONS ON THE WEB

If you have access to the Internet, try looking up these websites:

Enkosini Reserve
www.enkosini.com
This website is about the work of the Enkosini Reserve in South Africa, which is dedicated to the conservation of predators, especially lions.

Lion Research Center
www.w1.adhost.com/lionresearch/main.html
A website with plenty of factual information about lion behavior and research. Here you can listen to recordings of the lion's roar.

Asiatic Lion Conservation
www.asiatic-lion.org
This website focuses on the Asiatic lion. Here you will find lot of information on this lion and how it is being conserved.

Born Free Foundation
www.bornfree.org.uk
The Born Free Foundation is an international wildlife charity that aims to prevent cruelty and suffering to animals, especially zoo animals. It was set up by Virginia McKenna and Bill Travers, who starred in the film *Born Free*.

INDEX